The Hubbard Family of Kent England

by Lorine McGinnis Schulze

ISBN: 978-1-987938-13-5
Copyright 2017
All rights reserved
Publisher Olive Tree Genealogy

By Lorine McGinnis Schulze. http://OliveTreeGenealogy.com

Over the last 40 plus years I have researched and gathered a great deal of information and uncovered many documents for my mother's ancestors in England. Pondering how best to preserve my research and share the stories of these maternal ancestors, I decided to compile books on each family surname.

Because the books were written for family, I have not cited my sources nor have I written long chapters of anecdotal stories. Instead I opted to create a chronological timeline for each generation. Images for all baptismal, marriage, burial, land records and so on that were discovered for each ancestor are also included.

If siblings were found, family group sheets are included. If they were not found, only my direct ancestor is noted. At the end of the book you will find blank pages for your own notes.

Those who want to know my sources can contact me directly through my website Olive Tree Genealogy at www.OliveTreeGenealogy.com My email is found at the bottom of each page.

I hope that readers enjoy these books and the stories of the ancestors.

Lorine McGinnis Schulze

Table of Contents

Hubbard Family of Kent England

My Hubbard ancestry has been found in Dover Kent England as far back as Isaac Hubbard born circa 1675. Because of its position, Dover controls the English Channel. Julius Caesar tried to land at Dover during the Roman Invasion of 55 BC and it was the prime objective of the invasion plans of William the Conqueror, Napoleon and Hitler.

As well as the massive castle, Dover's history as a military and garrison town can be seen in the extensive remains of its Roman forts, Napoleonic forts and defences from both the World Wars.

The churches used by the Hubbard family in Dover were St. James and St. Mary the Virgin. St. James was built in the 11th century but was badly damaged in World War 1 and World War 2.

St. James now. By Stephen McKay, CC BY-SA 2.0,
https://commons.wikimedia.org/w/index.php?curid=13508508

St. Mary's Church Dover

Isaac Hubbard ca 1680-1721

Isaac Hubbard and Mary Ducy or Duty were married 13 November 1699 but nothing further is known of the couple although Mary was recorded as a widow in another entry for their marriage.

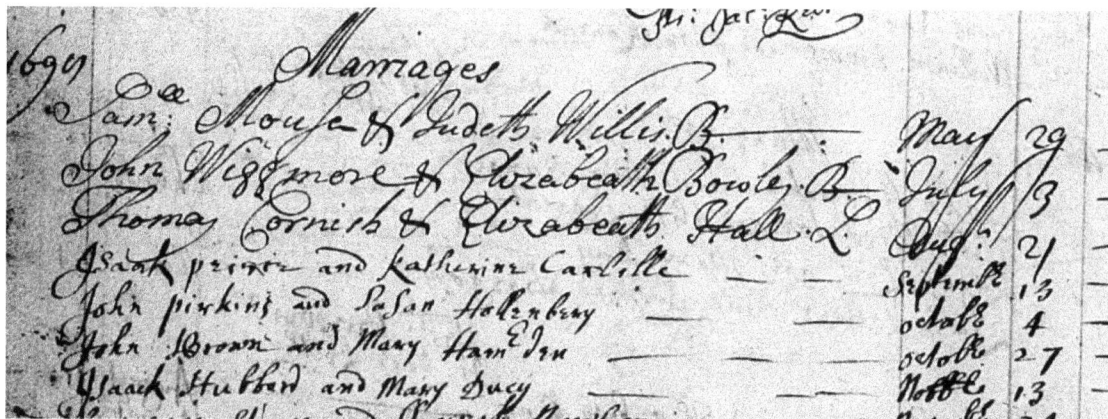

Mary Hubbard died in November 1707 leaving several small children, the youngest only 2 years old. Her name is found in the list of burials in St. Mary the Virgin church where the surname is spelled Hubbart.

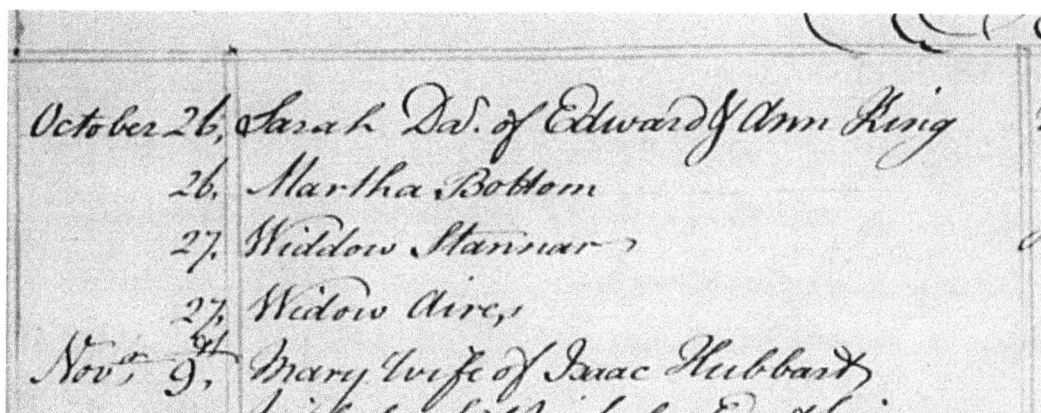

Isaac Sr. is found in St. Mary the Virgin's list of burials on 2 October 1721.

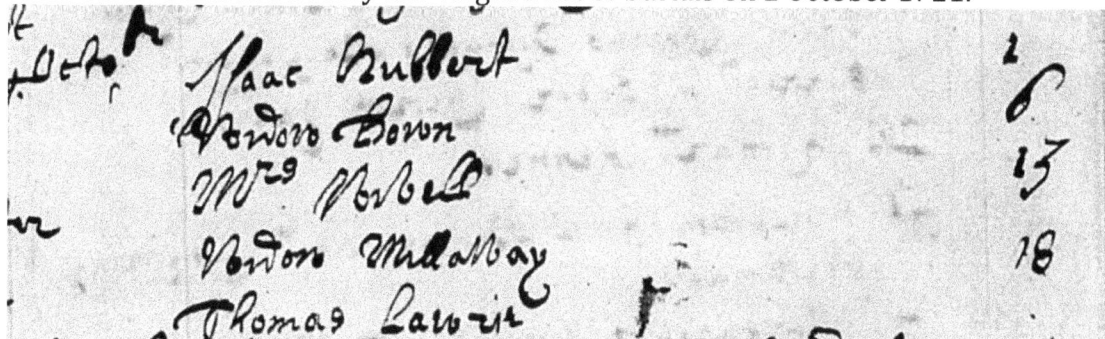

Isaac Hubbard 1701-

Isaac was baptised 18 May 1701 in St. Mary the Virgin, Dover England to parents Isaac Hubbard and Mary Ducy.

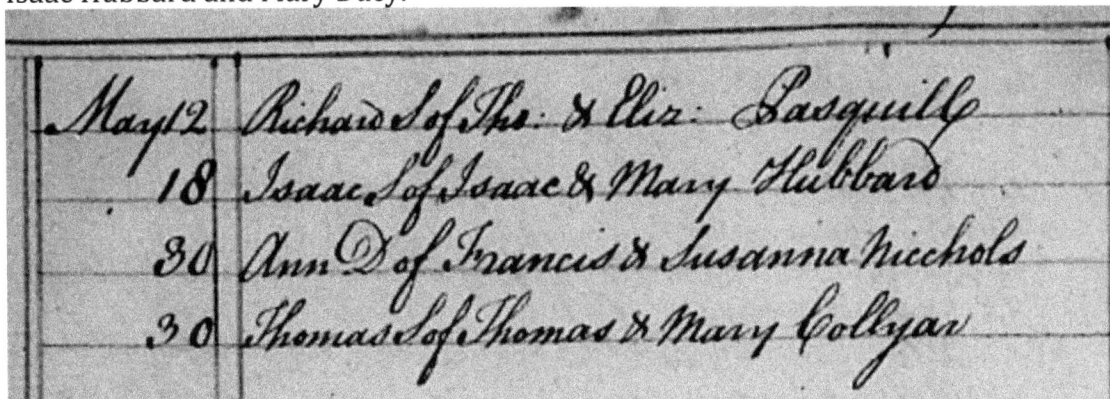

Isaac and Mary's son Isaac Hubbard Jr married Patience Badcock 7 September 1724 in Dover in St. Mary the Virgin.

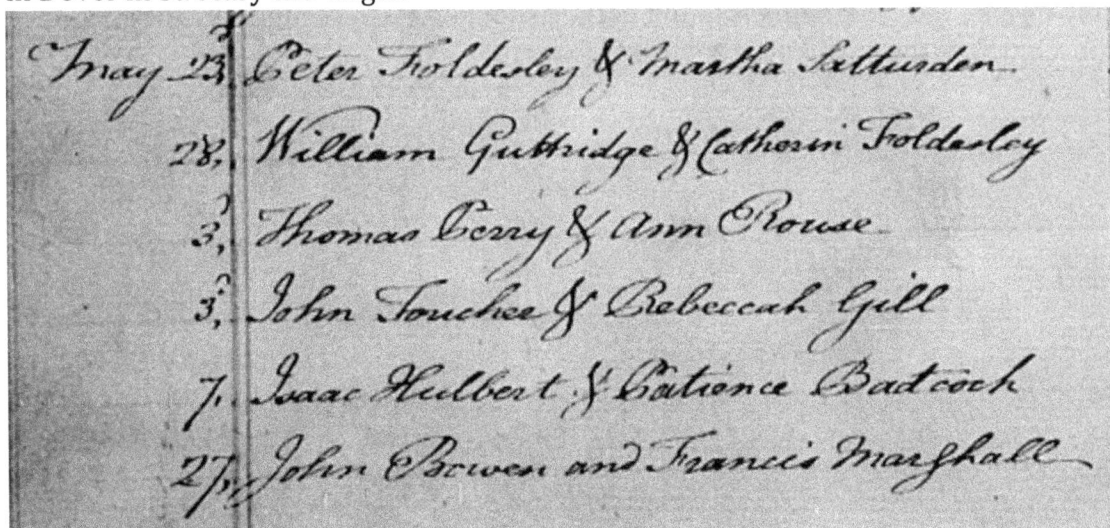

Patience was baptised 15 December 1697 in Folkestone, St Mary & St Eanswith, Kent. Her parents were recorded as George & Alice Badcock.

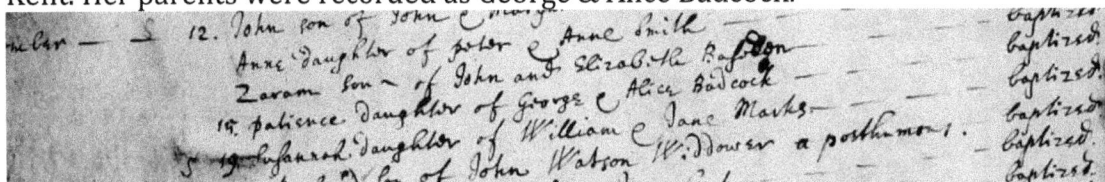

Patience's father George Badcock married Alice Penny in July 1685 in St. Margaret in Canterbury England. Both were noted as being from Folkestone. George's age was recorded as 25 and his occupation a husbandman. Alice was 20.

Kent, Canterbury Archdeaconry marriages 1538-1928

Both George and Alice lived to unusually old ages for the times! George died in 1742 and was noted as being over 80 years old, while Alice outlived him, dying in 1754 and noted as being 96 years old! Both were buried in Folkestone, SS Mary & Eanswith

1742 Burial of George Badcock, farmer aged above 80

1754 Burial of Alice Badcock, widow aged 96 years

By 28 April 1748 George and Alice Badcock's daughter Patience Hubbard was dead. Her burial is listed in St. Mary the Virgin's register.

Family Group Sheet for Isaac Hubbard

Husband:		Isaac Hubbard
	b:	18 May 1701 in Dover, Kent, Eng.
	m:	07 Sep 1724 in Dover, Kent England
	Father:	Isaac Hubbard
	Mother:	Mary Ducy or Duty
Wife:		Patience Badcock
	b:	15 Dec 1697 in Folkestone, Kent England
	d:	Apr 1748 in Dover Kent England
	Father:	George Badcock
	Mother:	Alice Penny

Children:		
1	Name:	Isaac Hubbard
M	b:	21 Jun 1725 in St. Mary the Virgin, Dover, Kent Eng
2	Name:	Philip Hubbard
M	b:	22 Feb 1730 in St. Mary the Virgin, Dover, Kent, Eng.
	m:	11 Jan 1752 in St. Mary, Dover, Kent, Eng
	Spouse:	Emblen Smithett
3	Name:	Mary Hubbard
F	b:	15 Jan 1731/32 in St. Mary the Virgin, Dover, Kent Eng
4	Name:	Abraham Hubbard
M	b:	28 Apr 1734 in St. Mary the Virgin, Dover, Kent Eng

Notes:

Philip Hubbard 1731-?

Patience and Isaac Hubbard's son Philip Hubbard was baptised 22 February 1731 at the age of 10 months, in St. Mary the Virgin.

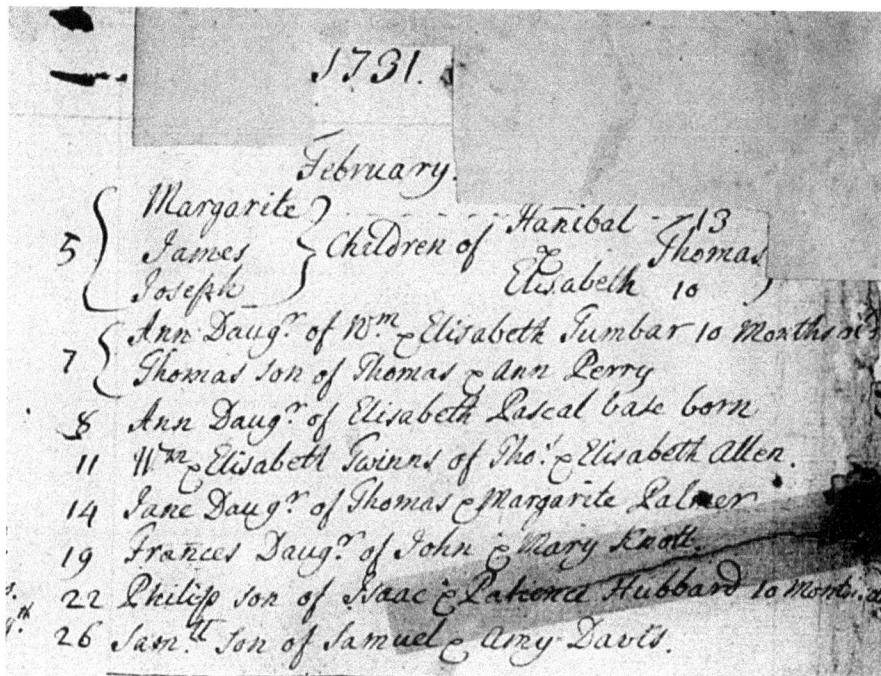

Philip married Emblen Smithett on 11 January 1752 in St. Mary the Virgin. Emblen was baptised in 1732 in the same church where she was married. Her parents were Thomas and Emblen (Pascall) Smithett.

Emblen came from a long line of Dover seamen, many of them pilots who guided incoming ships into Dover Harbour in the 17th century. Her father and maternal grandfather were Freemen of Dover, a very distinguished group with higher status and more privileges than the average townsperson.

Family Group Sheet for Philip Hubbard

Husband:		Philip Hubbard
	b:	22 Feb 1730 in St. Mary the Virgin, Dover, Kent, Eng.
	m:	11 Jan 1752 in St. Mary, Dover, Kent, Eng
	Father:	Isaac Hubbard
	Mother:	Patience Badcock
Wife:		Emblen Smithett
	b:	13 Mar 1732 in St. Mary the Virgin, Dover, Kent Eng
	Father:	Thomas Smithett
	Mother:	Emblen or Emeline or Emily Pascall
Children:		
1	Name:	Philip Hubbard
M	b:	08 Jan 1753 in Dover, Kent England
	m:	17 Oct 1787 in Saint Laurence, Thanet, Kent, Eng
	Spouse:	Elizabeth (Betsy) Moses Hinds
2	Name:	Isaac Hubbard
M	b:	10 Nov 1754 in Dover, Kent England
3	Name:	Emblen Hubbard
F	b:	14 Jun 1756 in Dover, Kent England
	d:	02 Feb 1759 in Dover, Kent England
4	Name:	William Hubbard
M	b:	26 Feb 1758 in Dover, Kent England
5	Name:	Emblen Hubbard
F	b:	03 Feb 1760 in Dover, Kent England
	d:	19 Jan 1764 in Dover, Kent England

Philip Hubbard 1753-?

My 5th great-grandfather Philip Hubbard was baptised in the same church one year later on 8 January 1753.

Apparently Philip was a Soap and Salt Merchant. The following ad was placed from February to May 1787 in the Kentish Gazette, Kent, England

On 08 May 1781 Philip married Mary Avent in St. Mary Major in Exeter Devon.

Three years later Mary died and was buried from the Anglican church of St. Thomas in Exeter on 26 September 1784.

On 17 October 1787 Philip, a widower, married Elizabeth (Betsy) Moses in St. Laurence, Thanet Kent. Their marriage was recorded as

Philip Hubbard, widower & Elizabeth Moses Burbank widow both of St. Laurence, Wit: Philip Hubbard & John Goss

Further checking of church records showed that Betsy Moses married Richard Burbank on 03 June 1785 in St. Laurence, Thanet, Kent.

In the register, Betsy is noted as Elizabeth Moses Hinds, spinster, while Richard is noted as a widower. It may be interesting to note that Richard had been previously married to Margaret, who died in 1784 and whose tombstone is found in the cemetery attached to the church of St Laurence in Thanet (Ramsgate).

John ROBERTS died 13th March 1741 aged 67 years. Also John Roberts COOPER, son of William and Margaret Cooper, died October 1779 aged 23 years. Also the above William Cooper died 10th September 1783 aged 67 years. Also Margaret, wife of Richard BURBANK, died 2nd June 1784 aged 33 years. Also the above Margaret Cooper died 29th December 1789 aged 67 years.

Richard Burbank's will was probated in 25 August 1785. He was a Mariner and Master of Ramsgate in the Isle of Thanet , Kent. It is likely that either Richard was ill or was about to embark on what he knew could be a dangerous voyage. In the will he names his wife Elizabeth Moses Burbank and his brother Robert Burbank, as well

as his sisters Ann Parrott, widow, Elizabeth Rolfe of Joseph Smith, Mary Rolfe of
John Hafford.

Estate with the appurtenances ... and all my said Monies Securities for money &c plate linnen & household furniture Effects goods & chattels and personal Estate whatsoever to all and every my child and children as well such as shall be born before my decease as after equally to be divided between such children if more than one and they to ... a take as Tenants in common and not as joint Tenants but if I shall leave no such child or children or if I shall leave any such child or children all such children shall happen to die under the age of twenty one years without leaving any lawful Issue of his her or their Bodies lawfully ... I give devise and bequeath all my said Messuages Lands Tenements Hereditaments and Real Estate and the Dividends Interest and profits of all my said Monies Securities for Money Effects or goods Chattels and personal Estate to my Brother and ... Sisters Robert Burbank John Parrett Widow Elizabeth wife of Joseph Smith and Mary wife of John Hafford for and during the term of their respective natural Lives ... and from and after their decease respectively I give ... devise and bequeath the same Messuages Lands ... Tenements Monies Securities and my said Real and ... personal Estates to all and every the Child and Children of my said Brother and Sister Robert Burbank and ... Parrett equally to be divided between them share and share alike and to their respective heirs Executors Administrators and Assigns to hold the same as Tenants in common and not as joint Tenants And I appoint my said Wife sole Executrix of this my last Will and Testament and do hereby revoke all former Wills by me made In witness whereof I have hereunto set my hand and seal this eighth day of June in the year of our Lord one thousand seven hundred and eighty five and in the twenty fifth year of the Reign of our sovereign Lord King George the third &c Rich[d] Burbank (seal) signed sealed published and declared by the said Richard Burbank the Testator as and for his last Will and Testament in the presence of us who have subscribed our names in his presence Richard Pearce Pilcher Longley, John Daniel

𝕿𝖍𝖎𝖘 𝖂𝖎𝖑𝖑 was proved at London the twenty fifth Day of August in the Year of our Lord one thousand seven hundred and eighty five before the Right ... Worshipful Peter Calvert Doctor of Laws Master &c Keeper or Commissary of the prerogative court of ... Canterbury lawfully constituted by the Oath of Elizabeth Burbank widow the Relict of the deceased and sole Executrix named in the said Will to whom Administration was granted of all and singular the goods Chattels and Credits of the said deceased she ...

she having been first sworn by commission duly to administer ...

In this church register, Elizabeth is clearly noted as a widow.

Elizabeth Moses Hind(s) was baptised in St. Lawrence, Thanet Kent on February 2, 1764 to John and Mildred Hind(s)

The five children of Philip Hubbard and Elilzabeth Moses Hinds were all baptised in St Lawrence in Thanet, Kent England

Family Group Sheet for Philip Hubbard

Husband:		Philip Hubbard
	b:	08 Jan 1753 in Dover, Kent, Eng.
	m:	17 Oct 1787 in Saint Laurence, Thanet, Kent, Eng
	Father:	Philip Hubbard
	Mother:	Emblen Smithett
Wife:		Elizabeth (Betsy) Moses Hinds
	b:	02 Feb 1764 in St Lawrence in Thanet, St Lawrence Kent
	Father:	John Hinds
	Mother:	Mildred Ellington
Children:		
1	Name:	Milly Elizabeth Hubbard
F	b:	27 Jul 1788 in Saint Laurence, Thanet, Kent, Eng
	m:	06 Jun 1805 in St. Laurence, Ramsgate, Kent Eng.
	d:	13 May 1871 in Ramsgate, Kent Eng
	Spouse:	John Caspall
2	Name:	Margaret Hubbard
F	b:	28 Jan 1790 in Saint Laurence, Thanet, Kent, Eng
3	Name:	Elizabeth Hubbard
F	b:	12 Oct 1791 in Saint Laurence, Thanet, Kent, Eng
	d:	Dec 1792 in Saint Laurence, Thanet, Kent, Eng
4	Name:	Elizabeth Hubbard
F	b:	05 Nov 1792 in Saint Laurence, Thanet, Kent, Eng
5	Name:	Mary Ann Hubbard
F	b:	24 Jun 1795 in Saint Laurence, Thanet, Kent, Eng

Milly Elizabeth Hubbard 1788-1871

Philip and Betsy's daughter Milly Elizabeth Hubbard was baptised in St. Laurence on 27 July 1788 and on 06 June 1805 she married John Caspall.

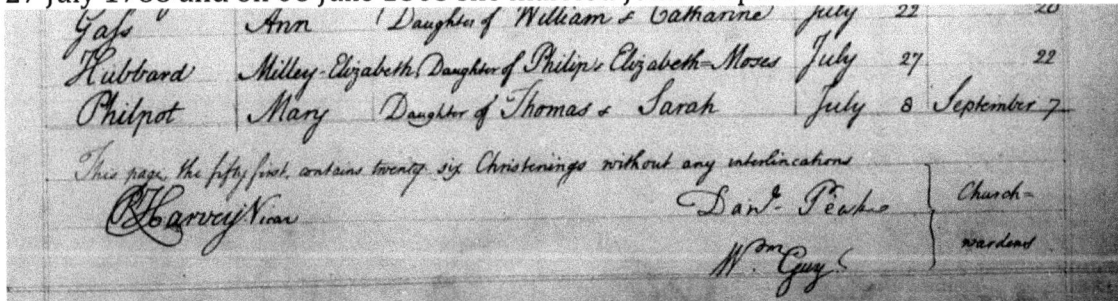

1788 Baptism of Milly Elizabeth Hubbard

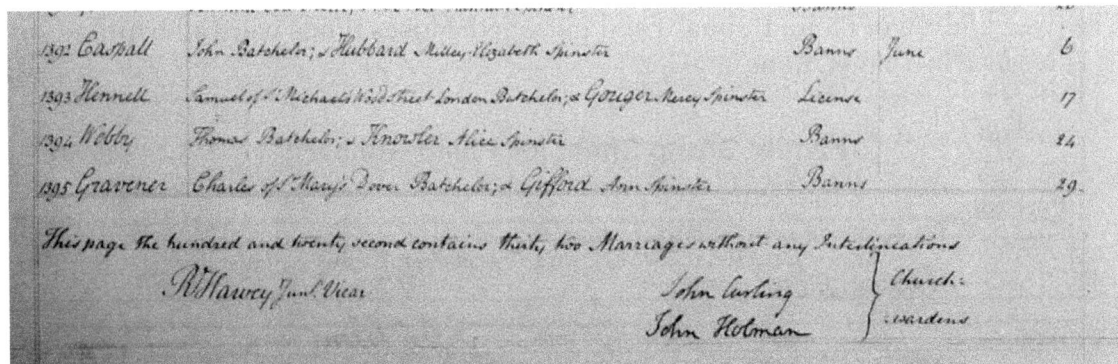

1805 Marriage of Milly Elizabeth Hubbard & John Caspall

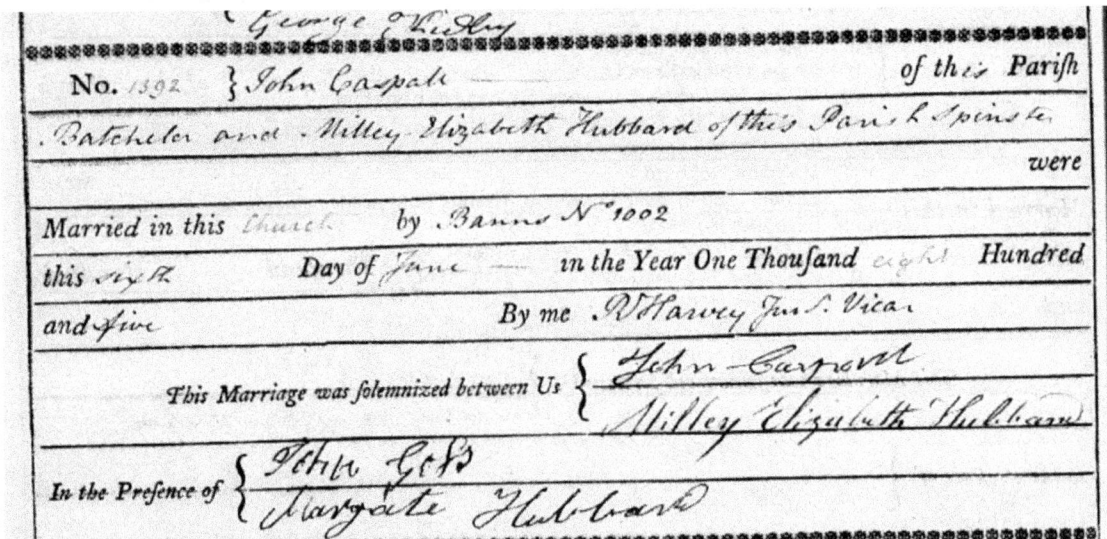

Notes

www.ingramcontent.com/pod-product-compliance
Lightning Source LLC
Chambersburg PA
CBHW051351290326
41933CB00043B/3451